I0491039

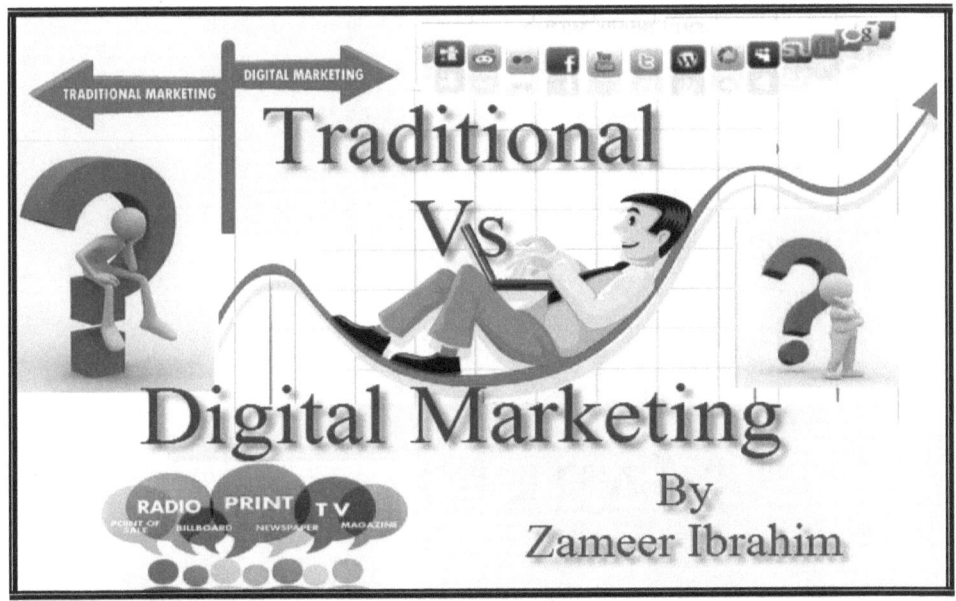

TRADITIONAL MARKETING

VS

DIGITAL MARKETING

By

Zameer Ibrahim

Disclaimer

This e-book has been written for information purposes only. However, by our experience, we have taken every effort to make this ebook as complete & accurate as possible.

Please excuse us for the typography errors or may be mistakes in content which unknowingly crept in. This ebook is with up to date information to the publishing date. Therefore, this ebook should be used as a guide.

To Educate friends is the only sole purpose of this ebook. Hence, the author and the publisher do not fully take warranty about the information contained in this e-book and shall not be responsible for any errors or omissions there on.

The author and publisher shall have neither liability nor responsibility to any person or entity with respect to any loss or damage caused or alleged to be caused directly or indirectly by this ebook.

TABLE OF CONTENTS

INTRODUCTION

1.1. JOHN AND TOM – TWO FRIENDS.

In 1990s, there were two children - John and Tom, 5 years of age. They were much close to each other.

John is from very well-known family of a businessman. They had a small shoe making traditional factory which his parents & grandparents ran & almost 100 people works in his Dad's factory. It was very famous shoe factory since last 80 years.

The factory was laid by his great grandfather few decades ago. People around the state used to come and buy various kinds of shoes in their factory outlet. Their order book was full of orders and was never empty.!!

Small shopkeepers, shoes sellers needed to book their orders in advance and they receive their products almost after waiting for a month or two. In short, the shoe factory was very prestigious, famous and admired not only in the state but also in the country..!!

Indeed, buying shoes from there was a prestigious thing for all people. It was situated near the bank of river where John and Tom grew up and now they were in their adolescent age.

Tom & John grew playing and roaming around the city together. John was hereditarily rich but his best friend Tom belongs to a middle class family. Tom's mom and dad were teachers in the Local City School.

The day came when John's father asked him to take the charge of the big, famous shoe factory. John happily joined his dad's traditional family business of shoe making in 2010 while Tom kept on studying and went to the University for Highest Studies.

Tom studied in university and John kept on running his traditional shoe factory successfully & proudly.

1.2 OPPOSITE YET CLOSE FRIENDS

Time flies like wind. They both met after almost 5 long years. Their friendship bloom in last 20 years and there wasn't a single day when both of them didn't talk or chat with each other.

Tom completed his degree in Computer engineering and joined a fortune 500 Software company in nearby city.

John kept on managing his traditional company successfully. They both were busy in their daily routine lives still they usually meet on every weekend.

They used to go on their hiking safari on long islands, sometimes go fishing on the river and keep mum for hours just catching fishes.

They were very close to each other. However, there was a small gap of 5 years between them when Tom was away for his studies in the University and John was also tied up with the neck cutting competitions between the newly arriving shoe manufacturing companies around.

He was not at all a person who sticks to the traditions unnecessarily. He ran his hereditary and ancient shoe manufacturing factory proudly. In his undertakings, he made lot of changes in the department structures, brought new machineries, technologies and also visited other countries to see the shoe manufacturing progress in other nations.

Since childhood, Tom was a genius student and has a blessed grasping & analysis power inherited by his parents who were teachers.

He also got engaged in his new role in the company as a digital marketing expert for the software company. His company helps other client companies to increase their sells via digital marketing & to bring their presence on the Digital World's era.

They both were catching fish but quietly glance and admire each other when the other one is busy fishing.

1.3 THE CLOUDS OF PROBLEM

After few months, one day John called Tom in the morning when Tom was just about to go for an important meeting.

There was a deep concern and worry in John's voice. Tom understood that something is wrong with John. Tom agreed to meet immediately but John said lets meet in the evening.

That evening, taking seep of coffee, they both were sitting in John's big office from where they saw the sunset hundreds of time since they were children.

But today is a different time. John looked totally disturbed and that made Tom worry about him more. Silently they finished their coffee.

Tom asked him what happened and why he looked so worried and tensed.

John told Tom everything that is going on in his factory since last few years.

How their sales started going down, how all of sudden skilled people started leaving, buyers drastically reducing their orders.

Moreover, their prestigious name started falling down in market and lot of people started buying shoes from other manufacturers in the market.

John was totally disturbed when he saw that the quality of shoes made in his factory is really very high compared to the new manufactures arrived recently in the market since few years.

John told him about the degrading financial situation of the factory and he exclaimed the threat in his mind that comes very often – *what if I have to close down the factory?*

Tom understood the situation is very serious and how John spent sleepless nights just thinking over and over again about the degrading situation of his Factory.

Tom was equally worried but he told John not to have anxiety. They sat for few minutes in silence. John looked helpless and Tom was in deep thinking.

Tom inquired about the employees and their skills. John said he has total faith in all of the team like Production, Purchase, packaging and marketing! Many employees are there since more than last 10 years. They are very skilled and acquired great knowledge in shoes manufacturing using latest technologies.

John further said all department heads are well aware of their responsibilities. Marketing team was doing flawless marketing according to their traditional business strategy.

Tom's eyes were sparkling after few moments.

Tom said, "**Anything new you added recently to improve your degrading sell?**"

John said, "**We all are very much open to new production ideas as you saw the new technology implemented in our factory..**"

To which Tom replied, "**Anything new in marketing department..?**"

John, "**No..! Not at all..! Why we need to change it ..? As we are using Well established and proven strategies of Traditional Marketing since long..**"

Tom said ok and he was staring at John as if he is looking through his heart.

John then replied in sad tone that it's his and company's fate that is taking them down. They are totally confused and eventually can do nothing to save his factory!!

Tom nodded and looked at John and said he shall meet after 3-4 days with something concrete plan in hand. Before leaving for his house Tom told John to gather and prepare the entire data of last 5 years. Get it done from all his managers.

He asked him to get the reports & data ready from all the related department heads like marketing, purchase and sales, etc,. Then he asked John to arrange an important meeting after 4 days with all department heads & managers. John felt confused but still he nodded. At last Tom is the only best friend he got.

1.4 CHALLENGES, CHALLENGES, CHALLENGES

4 Days later, the main meeting room looked like a war room!! All department heads were about to gather there. The meeting will commence in any minute from now. All the managers were curious and yet little tensed. Nobody knows why they are asked to gather like this.

Few of them started thinking about lay-off declaration in this meeting and that's why their faces were looking pale. Praying God they should stay back in company.

Tom came with his laptop and bunch of papers. He started the meeting exactly sharp at 9:00 am. They all were busy in the meeting till lunch.

All managers were exhausted while answering questions asked by Tom. He collected all the reports, asked hundreds of questions and his face started to show worried expressions and then he left with John for lunch.

All managers felt a relief when they both went. Nobody got fired..!!

Tom told John about the new marketing strategy that he must adhere to.

It is called Digital Marketing Strategy.

He explained in detail and suggested every possible way and told John about the latest marketing technique which is Digital Marketing and how he must follow it to increase the sell and save the factory by shutting it down.

John looked at Tom with great surprise. He was totally against this new thing coming up in the market. He showed no interest in Tom's theory. He was listening with closed mind since beginning.

John refuted…

He said, **"It's only a THEORY of so called Digital Revolution..**
Nothing is going to change. I have no rights to take this new threat upon my factory because its already going down."

John said, **"This is NOT the RIGHT TIME to try anything new..!"**

Further he said the possibility of shutting down the company is really going high.

John and his honest, learned, skilled managers and department heads were trying all possible ways to do marketing the same way they are doing since many years..!!

Tom was shocked by John's speech.. But he did not interfere till he finish.

John was very adamant and Tom had to apply great efforts in making him understand about what is Digital Marketing. He was thinking on the ways how should he ask him to implement in his factory.

He quietly but very firmly said one word by one word, **"John, THIS is THE RIGHT TIME to implement this new thing called Digital Marketing in your facyory..!"**

He tried to convince John from his depth of heart and said, **"This is the only way to stop the losses and start getting new customers and new business."**

1.5 STRONG REFUTE

John was not at all ready to listen what Tom has to say. He showed no temperament of accepting anything new at this Risky stage.

He said, "**Tom, were my father & grandfather mad..?**

They ran this factory on Traditional business strategies which are there before we were born.. !!

Traditional business marketing strategies are long established and very strong since time immemorial.. You also knew this..!

Our factory is been running strongly on these strategies since a century now... How come anything new comes up just like that which you claim is the BEST Today..?

I don't trust this…not at all…!!

I don't even think of it and any of its value addition over traditional business strategies..! "

Tom felt worried because he understood the flaw in John's traditional ways of marketing..! The root cause of John's degradation is what he witnessed by his own eyes..!

He thought to himself that John still needs very big attention to understand the Digital theory which is going to be the fact of the era..!!

Later he looked deep in John's eyes and said firmly,

"Let's go back to your office and then I will show you few realities which are unbelievable... and these theories will become FACTS soon..!"

"And.... If you trust me John.. this is the only way to save your factory...!!"

John kept on looking at Tom and said nothing.

WHAT IS TRADITIONAL MARKETING?

They reached John's office and then Tom pulled his laptop in front of him and started showing few graphs to John.

Tom said, **"Dear John, now look closely..! Here are few details I am going to show you.. Just take a close look at it and try to understand with an open mind.. "**

Let's start from the beginning…

Here are few graphs which show details of traditional Marketing ways of Business..!

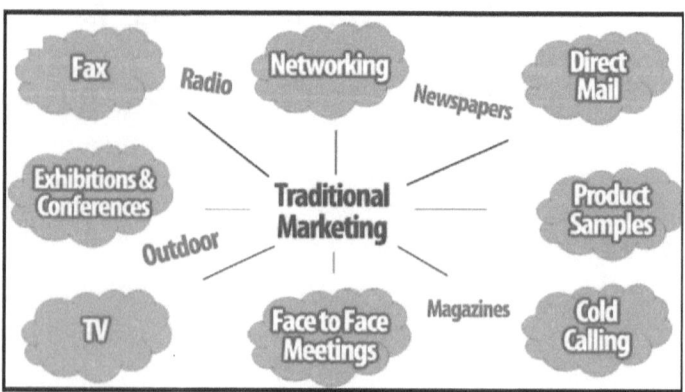

2.1 Traditional Marketing:

It is the way of doing marketing with the available media (which was print media) in those days when these strategies were introduced.

The main strategies basically includes:-

1. Face To Face Meetings
2. Door-to-door Marketing
3. Exhibitions & Conferences
4. Distributing Product samples
5. Print Media (Sending Postcards, Newspaper ads, Newsletters, ads in Magazines, exchanging Business Cards, Circulating Pamphlets, handouts, Brochures, etc,.)
6. Electronic Media (TV ads, Radio jingles)
7. MLM, Network Marketing
8. Fax & Cold calling, telemarketing
9. Putting ads on big hoardings on highway, billboards, etc,.
10. Others

Then Tom turned to John and asked, **"Am I missing anything that your traditional business used John..?"**

John looked closely and said, **"Nah.. All major marketing strategies that we are using since ages are listed..!"**

Tom further said, "**These are the main widely used Traditional strategies we know... these were strong, proved by time, well thoughtfully established and nobody didn't require to change anything so far....**"

Since they were invented, they had a proven techniques and very high success rates, long standing initiatives that common public already understands.

The great challenge in Traditional Marketing Strategy was measuring success rate!

Measuring success rate is really difficult in traditional businesses... Assume that you spend $1000 per month to put up an ad on a roadside billboard.

Do you have any way to find out how many people buy your products by looking at that ad?

You really have no way to know how many people saw the particular ad on that hoarding. Same goes with Newspaper ads...

You have no idea how many of those people purchased a product in your store after reading newspaper ads or viewing the lovely lady on your hoarding's ad.!!

John nodded unknowingly.

Tom continued his explanations further…

He said, "**These are too costly ways of Traditional Business ads.. Moreover, its really difficult to find out the success rate from such costly print media ads..**"

2.2 DRAWBACKS

Few of the Drawbacks are:-

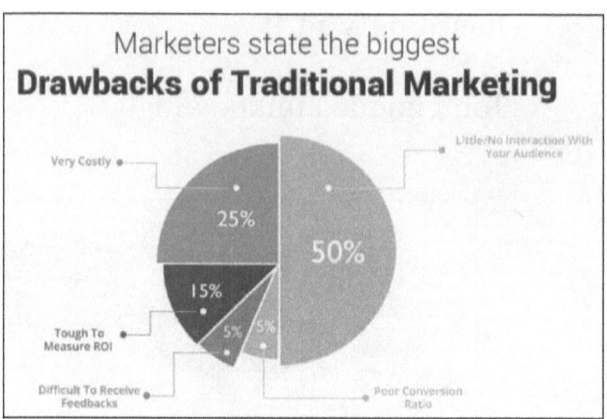

As shown in the graph above, basically there are below major drawbacks seen in the traditional ways of marketing in today's era:-

1. These ad publishers for eg. Newspaper owners, billboard owners, etc,. Did not reduce their cost of putting ads. Almost 25%

2. Very difficult to measure the Rate Of Interest of readers / viewers almost 15%.

3. It is difficult to receive feedbacks from viewers. Almost 5%. You do not know if they have any genuine

valuable suggestion about the product.

4. No interaction happens between the product company and the viewers / readers. There was no way to get the improvement ideas of what people wants from their product. Almost 50%

5. Conversion ratio from 'Viewing to buying' was just 5%.

John looked confused. He said, "Tom, are you sure about these statistics..?"

Tom smiles and said, "Yes bro... I am very much sure about these stats shown here as they are taken from the world famous Reuters association's website."

John then looked lost in the thinking process. Tom did not disturb him... he was busy in his laptop finding another graph to show..

After sometime, John said in slow tone, "I think you are right Tom.. We never used to know whether our ads are having expected impact on the buyers.. We failed to understand them.."

Tom then continued,

"Yes.. John... It is really difficult to get the buyers feedback in this way..

2.3 CHOOSING THE RIGHT ONE

Tom further said, **"Choosing the right one is really a difficult task. It totally depends on the type of business you run."**
If you are well informed, well understood of this book then it won't be difficult for you to choose the path that is right for you.

With Digital or Online Marketing, with the accurately chosen ways with right tools & comparatively low cost platform, below questions are answered:-

1. How many viewers saw your posts?

2. How many of them saw your ads, or videos?

3. How many of those visited your brand's online presence i.e. website?

4. You can even see how many of those bought your product?

5. How many are happy with the products?

6. How many of them put positive feedback about your service?

Tracking Digital Marketing Efforts means very important thing called opportunity for second sell which also means:-

- Measure the entire traffic to your site.
- How much time they spent on your website before they purchase?
- Did they leave without purchase?
- How much is your audience's engagement on your social networks or website?
- You can even count the people visiting your blog and send them personal wishes birthday or anniversary cards and maintain long-term relationships with them.

This is the important part of **C.R.M. (Customer Relationship Management)** It makes easy to track and measure specific goals for your marketing efforts!! In other words, **IT'S VALUE FOR MONEY..!**

2.4 THE RAZOR SHARP EDGE

It is indeed like walking on a double edged razor sharp sword...

But, of course, that edge takes you to the TARGET i.e. SALE..!!!

Customer Relationship Management's very important fact is your customer must be satisfied with whatever you are selling him / her. This is 100% achievable in Digital Marketing Platform very easily.

It's like an eagle which never let go his eyes off the prey. Literally, following the buyer till their satisfaction level.

In short, here is a simple, easy and understandable image that explains the walk through between the traditional marketing and digital marketing.

It becomes easy to track the tentative buyer from the moment he / she lands on your website till they exits, of course, with your product…! ☺

Another important factor of digital marketing is – the feature of **'Call for action'** availability.. It gives you a chance to bring back the tentative buyer who left without buying anything..!

That means SECOND
OPPORTUNITY FOR SELL..!!

2.5 THE COMPARISON

John now started listening to Tom more carefully. Tom felt happy for John as he saw some sparkling hope in his eyes..!

Tom understood that he has to show the easy and simple comparison between the two.

So here it is:-

COST OF ADS

Tom proceeded to the next point – **Cost of ads..!**

The graph below is self-explanatory.

The difference is huge between the Cost to reach 2000 Audience in Traditional marketing and Digital Marketing.

Figures taken from the survey done from 2013 – 2019.

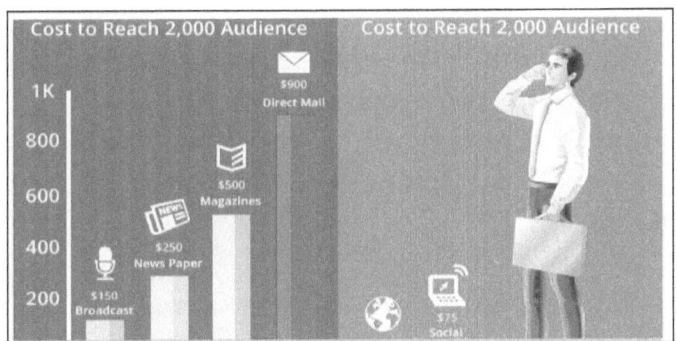

In the long run, keeping customers satisfied, holding them happy and making them revisit your website and increase the sell are the next important things in any company's growth in today's world!!

Reduce the cost on marketing yet keep the customers engage is the key for today's digital marketing which unfortunately did not available in the traditional marketing strategies.

So in short, when you have one customer, it is mandatory for any seller to keep that customer happy and must implement ways to bring them back again and again to your website's 'buyer page'. Digital tracking ways make it easy for every company!

Tom started feeling enthusiastic as John looked positive to him.
John said, "**Tom, you are really more than a brother to me..!**"

Now, I am started feeling hopeful and relaxed with this explanation..!
I have a doubt here.. I am little skeptical if this is beneficial to my shoe factory business...??"

Tom said, "**Certainly.. It will benefit to your old, existing customers... yet it will attract new customers from around the globe.."**

"Once you have appearance on internet...it reaches to the corners of the world.. You may get orders from around the globe for your shoes.!!"

3.1 THE WORLD IS NOT ENOUGH

"John, Just look at the below image..!!!"

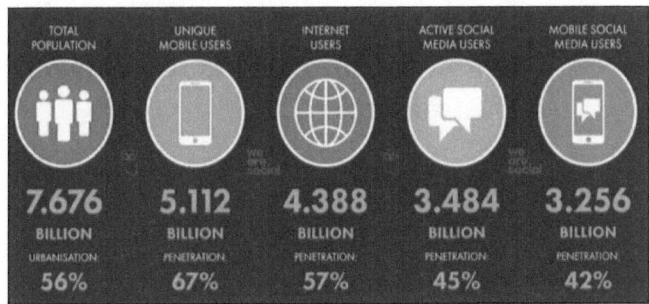

The internet is spreading very faster all over the world. The above image is taken from the best trusted site - **Forbes**!

It clearly says that the 57% of the entire world population uses internet on their desktop or laptop. Social media users are almost 45% worldwide which keep searching, buying, and using various products all the time.

"Are they enough to buy your shoes John..?"

John laughed and said,

"This is really unbelievable... but yes Tom, you are right.. I must adhere to the new marketing strategies of today's

age if I want to double, triple my business...

I don't worry about quality of my product as it's the best..

Now I am curious to attract global customers.."

3.2 ECOMMERCE GROWTH WORLDWIDE

John was happily surprised to look at the below mentioned percentages.

It shows the growth rate worldwide..!!

Never before rate of growth i.e. 23% every year worldwide is really unbelievable rate of growth.!

John was shocked when he read **"37% of online spending in Europe and the USA is made through Amazon alone..!!"**

3.3 FACEBOOK, AMAZON, GOOGLE EARNINGS

To surprise him more Tom gave him the latest data of the world's top richest companies for 2019.

Google, Facebook, Alibaba, Amazon & Ebay.

Tom told John to look below latest data:-

Facebook:- On Wednesday **8th January 2020**, reported advertising revenue at **$16.6 billion** for the **final quarter of last year**, up 30 percent year-over-year.

Total revenue earned during the quarter was $16.9 billion, with daily active users (DAU) at 1.52 billion, up 9 percent year over year

Amazon:- reported earnings for its third fiscal quarter of 2019, including revenue of **$70.0 billion, net income of $2.1 billion**, and earnings per share of $4.23 (compared to revenue of $56.6 billion, **net income of $2.9 billion**, and earnings per share of $5.75 in Q3 2018)

Alibaba Group: The statistic shows the annual revenue of the Alibaba Group from 2010 to 2019. In the fiscal year ending March 31, 2019, Chinese e-commerce corporation Alibaba recorded consolidated revenues of **376.8 billion** yuan. This translates to approximately 54.5 billion U.S. dollars

Google: In the third quarter of 2019, Google's revenue amounted to **40.3 billion U.S.D**, up from 38.8 billion U.S. dollars in the preceding quarter. Google's main revenue source is advertising through Google sites and its network.Nov 19, 2019

3.4 5 RICHEST MEN OF 2019

Tom said, -

"According to Forbes magazine, there are FIVE Richest people In the LIST of world's TOP 10 RICHEST People are from Internet Digital World..!!

John's eyes popped out and he dropped his jaw in utter surprise..!!!

Tom laughed looking at John.

John then insisted to show more about this internet virtual world where multiple benefits are hidden.

He thought to himself that it's like a Hidden Treasure full of Gold, Silver, Platinum, Diamonds and what not..!

The one who awakes and takes advantage of it, shall dig the treasure of Gold for unlimited time..

Surprisingly, this Gold mine is not reserved for any race, clan, any color, anyone..!!

It's open for ALL OF US..!! We just
need to FOCUS and DIG DEEP with
our knowledge and experience of others
who explains..!!

There are opportunities and chances for
hard and smart workers to become the
6th richest person in the world..!!!

Who knows, history is the only witness,
how a normal looking, poor and middle
class people like Jack Ma, Jeff Bezos,
Mark Zuckerberg, etc,. Climbed the
ladders of richness and success in last
few years.

They worked very hard but used smart
ways and used their intellectual
visionaries to see what was calling them
from the Horizon of the Internet world.!!

3.5 GOLD MINE

Tom explained,

"John, now see below are the graphs taken from Reuters and royal society of London..!"

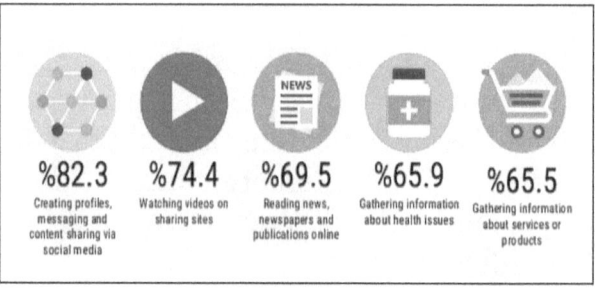

This is the graph that shows what people around the world are doing round the clock i.e. 24 x 7 x 365 days..!!

1. 82.3 % people create profile, busy in messaging others, content sharing via social media sites. Increase their friend lists.

2. 74.4% people watch videos on vdo sharing sites.

3. 69.5% people read newspapers, publications, eBooks etc,.

4. 65.9% people are collecting information about health issues and how to improve health.

5. 65.5% people gather information about services & products.

SOCIAL MEDIA USAGE

Today's world is a digital technology world where everyone either wants to show they are very much in limelight or they want to earn a lot from this wave of Gold Mine.

If someone wants to stay more luxurious than the current financial situation then it's the demand of Time. Also, if some 2-3 hours' work from home shall get you USDs then it's always better to bag it.!!

Below is the detailed study charts that explains today's digital world is going with supersonic speed and they are increasing.

4.1 INCREASING SOCIAL MEDIA USAGE

Below is the Business to Business content marketing social media platform usage in last few years:-

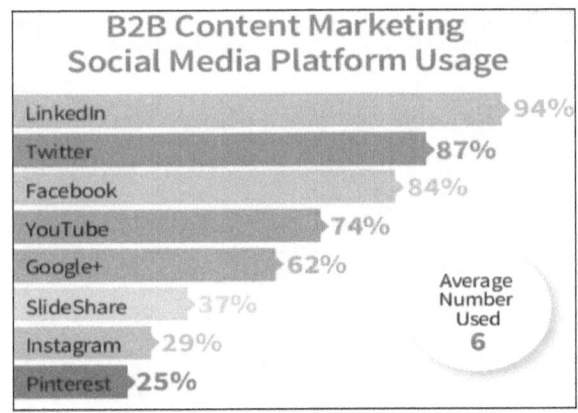

1. 94% People are getting hired using the site called LinkedIn.

2. 87% people are busy tweeting some or the other things on Twitter.

3. 84% people are using Facebook to either do social media appearances or to do marketing their products or just to earn money by PPC and other ways of marketing.

4. 74% People are busy in enjoying youtube vods

5. 62% people use google

6. 37% are using slideshare, 29% using instagram and 25% uses Pinterest..!

4.2 MOBILE AD REVENUE - 2019

Below is the Chart that shows US Market 2013 – 2018 revenue in Billion USDs..!!

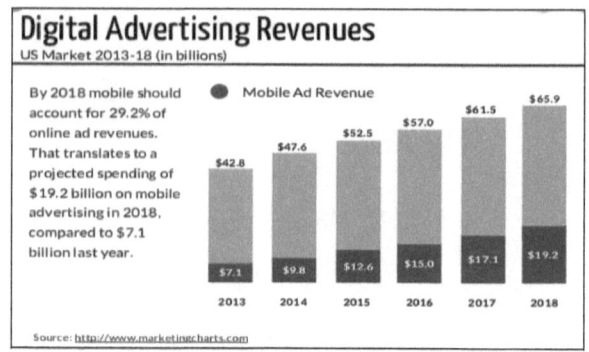

Below chart shows how much is the budget many big companies kept separate for online marketing presence.

4.3 HAPPY ENDING

Tom looked at John. He looked totally impressed.

Tom, "**John, as you have seen, these are not only theories, these are the facts since a decade now..!**

I don't have to tell you what to do now... To save your degrading shoe factory, what you must do..?"

John said, "**I am totally convinced by myself Tom..! I just have two words to say THANK YOU"**

Then they both smiled at each other.

Tom, "**Anytime John, we are brothers since childhood and I am equally happy to see your acceptance of Digital Marketing as a new strategy"**

John, "**now what Tom..?"**

Tom, "**Let's focus one by one..."**

I have a plan which is very simple to understand and easy to implement for everyone.

It works for both, who wants to run their small business of no employees or wants to run a big factory like you..!!

Just stick to the Plan that I will share in my next book..!"

Now you have learnt that you must choose and chase the Digital World Marketing Strategies over Traditional Marketing Strategies.

As shown in below figure, you shall also learn when to use the mixed marketing strategy i.e. how and when to mingle traditional and digital strategy.

www.ingramcontent.com/pod-product-compliance
Lightning Source LLC
Chambersburg PA
CBHW030541220526
45463CB00007B/2925